1 PETER

FOLLOWING JESUS

10 Publishing
a division of 10 of those.com

First published in Great Britain in 2017

British Library Cataloguing in Publication Data

A record for this book is available from the British Library

ISBN: 978-1-911272-22-9
Designed by Diane Warnes
Printed in the UK

10Publishing, a division of 10ofthose.com
Unit C, Tomlinson Road, Leyland, PR25 2DY, England
Email: info@10ofthose.com
Website: www.10ofthose.com

J. Marsden

48 UNDATED DEVOTIONS THROUGH THE BOOK OF 1 PETER

DAY 1 INTRODUCTION TO PETER'S FIRST LETTER

How do you find living as a Christian at the moment? There is much that is wonderful about being a Christian, but there is much that is hard too.

Everyone experiences difficulties in life, but becoming a Christian can add a whole set of extra ones. At times we may wonder if we will be able to keep going at following Christ. Will it all be worth it?

The letter we are going to read was written by Peter, one of Jesus' first followers. Peter's own Christian life had had its problems and pressures – and failures too. Peter knew first-hand that all of us need God's grace and help to keep going in following Jesus.

Peter's readers were Christians living in the first-century Middle East. They were facing all kinds of difficulties as well. It wasn't just one thing that was troubling them; Peter says that they 'have had to suffer grief in *all kinds* of trials' (1:6, my italics). Some of these trials were happening to them just because they were Christians.

Have a look at these snapshots from different parts of Peter's letter. How many of these difficulties can you identify with?

- These Christians were being insulted because of the name of Christ (4:14).
- People were speaking maliciously against them (3:16).
- They were being falsely accused of doing wrong (2:12).
- People thought the way they lived was strange (4:4).

Some of these Christians also had close family members who did 'not believe the word', with all the heartache and tensions that can bring (3:1). Peter's readers faced opposition in the spiritual realm too. Their enemy, the devil, was prowling around 'like a roaring lion looking for someone to devour' (5:8).

And these Christians still had 'sinful desires' raging in their own hearts – waging war against their souls (see 2:11). Even their fellow Christians brought them grief at times. Why else would Peter need to urge his friends to 'love *each other* deeply, because love covers over *a multitude of sins*' (4:8, my italics)?

These believers were certainly experiencing *all kinds* of trials. Would they keep going as Christians? Peter writes to help them to do just that. Peter's words can help us too.

PRAY

Talk to God about your own trials and griefs, especially those that have come your way because you are a Christian. Ask God to help you keep going in following Christ.

DAY 2

READ 1 Peter 5:12

Before we start reading Peter's letter from the beginning, we are going to look at one verse right at its end. Here Peter tells these stressed and suffering Christians what he hopes his letter will do for them. This verse tells us what this letter can do for us too. Peter writes:

With the help of Silas, whom I regard as a faithful brother, I have written to you briefly, encouraging you and testifying that this is the true grace of God. Stand fast in it (1 Pet. 5:12).

- ***Peter says he has been doing two things in his letter. What are they?***

When we are finding things tough, we need someone to come alongside us and encourage us. Peter wants to spur these believers on to keep going. He has also been telling them why it is so important that they do.

'Testifying' sounds like something you might do in a law court under oath. It means declaring something is really true, whatever anyone else may say. Peter has been writing about Jesus and about following him. He wants to reassure his friends and convince them all over again. This gospel about Jesus really is the only way to experience God's grace.

- ***What does Peter also call on his Christian friends to do?***

Embracing this gospel will bring suffering as well as joy now, but these believers mustn't be thrown off course. They *are* on the right track. There are always counterfeit 'gospels' around that offer an easier path through life. But these counterfeits will not bring us God's grace. As rebellious sinners deserving God's judgment, we need God's grace so much.

Peter's readers had already received 'the true grace of God'. The gospel about Jesus' death and resurrection had been preached to them. They had been born again spiritually as they came to believe in Jesus. We will read all about that in chapter 2.

So they have begun as Christians. These believers have taken their stand on the great truths of the gospel of Jesus. But they must also 'stand fast' in 'the true grace of God' as the pressures mount. It is the only way they, and we, will stay safe in eternity.

PRAY

Pray that this letter would encourage you and reassure you that the gospel is 'the true grace of God' so that you do 'stand fast in it'.

DAY 3

READ 1 Peter 1:1

Who do you listen to? We are surrounded by people who want our attention: people in our families; people in politics; people in the media. How do you choose which voices you will pay attention to and trust?

Why should we listen to Peter, a man who lived so long ago and far away? The answer is in the very first few words of his letter: Peter is 'an apostle of Jesus Christ'.

An 'apostle' is a person who has been sent by another to speak and act for them. Peter had been given authority by the Lord Jesus and sent out to speak for him. So the words of this letter are what Jesus himself wants to say to his followers. We need to listen up!

- ***The way Peter describes his readers is also very significant. What is the first thing Peter says about these Christians (v. 1)?***

'Elect' is another word for chosen. In an election you choose the person you want. To be a Christian is to be one of God's chosen ones. That is a very great privilege.

- ***But how else does Peter describe these believers here?***

These believers are wanted by God. They often feel unwanted though by the unbelievers they live amongst. It is hard to feel at home amongst people who reject Jesus. As Christians we can often feel like outsiders. You probably know something of how that feels.

Peter's readers aren't even all together as one people. At the moment they are scattered all over the ancient near east. But these believers are exiles or strangers in this world *because* they belong somewhere else. They feel the pain of being a scattered minority now *because* one day God will gather all his people together into one community. That day is coming.

For now, though, to be a Christian is to be an exile, a stranger in the world. How will they, and we, cope with the stress that can bring? When we feel rejected by those around us, we need to hold on to the fact that God himself has chosen us. There is great strength and great reassurance in knowing that. Keep it in your mind today.

PRAY

Ask God to help you to remember that he has chosen you to belong to him, especially when you feel like an exile, a stranger in the world.

DAY 4

READ 1 Peter 1:2

Today Peter will show you your purpose in life. God does have a purpose for your life and it is good for you to know it. This is especially true on days when you may feel your life is a bit aimless, or on days when your mind is full of all sorts of goals you have made up for yourself.

Yesterday we read that Peter called these scattered, stressed Christians 'God's elect'. Peter now goes on to tell these believers more about this truth.

- ***What has God chosen these believers to be (v. 2)?***

God's purpose for our lives is that we should be holy people who obey Jesus Christ. 'Sprinkled with ... blood' is picture language from the Old Testament for cleansing from sin through sacrifice. Through Jesus' sacrificial death, believers are cleaned up spiritually and made holy, ready for God's special purposes.

What is his purpose? God didn't choose us just so he could put our names on some list he keeps in heaven. God chose us so that we could begin to live obeying Jesus as Lord. That is what God wants you to do today.

- ***What does this verse tell us about how God chose these believers?***

God made a plan. Before the creation of the world, God made a plan to rescue a people to belong to him. These Christians have always been in God's mind to be part of this plan. That is the sense of the phrase 'according to the foreknowledge of God the Father'. It has the idea of making a plan in advance. Right back then, God decided that he wanted us in his family.

This wasn't because of all the good things we had done: that would make us feel very insecure, especially on our bad days. In fact, we hadn't done anything at all when God chose us; we hadn't even been born. God's plan to choose us has always been fixed and certain. There is great comfort and security in that.

God put his plan into action through Jesus' death and also 'through the sanctifying work of the Spirit'. To 'sanctify' means to set apart, to make holy. It is as if the Spirit had put his hand on these Christians' heads and said, 'You are mine.' If you are a believer today, that has happened to you too.

PRAY

Ask God to help you see the wonder of all this and to obey Jesus today.

DAY 5

READ 1 Peter 1:3–4a

'Well, that changes everything ...' We sometimes say that about some momentous event. In our verses today, Peter reflects on the event which really did change everything.

As Peter reflects, a great cry of adoration and worship rises up within him: 'Praise be to the God and Father of our Lord Jesus Christ!' (v. 3). As we read on, let's pray that our hearts would be stirred in the same way.

Peter praises God because he has given us 'new birth'. A mother *gives* birth to a baby. When you were a baby, you were on the receiving end of that experience. That is how your physical life began. The same is true of your spiritual life. It begins with a 'new birth' and that new birth is a gift.

Lots of privileges may belong to a baby just because he or she has been born into a particular family. The same is true of believers.

- ***When God gave you new birth, what two things were you born into?***

You have been born into an inheritance (v. 4). An inheritance is wealth which is yours. You may not have this wealth yet, but it will certainly be yours one day.

You have also been born into something which you do experience now. You have been born into a 'living hope' (v. 3). Believers have been born into a new life which is filled with hope. We live every day knowing for certain that we will live forever with Christ.

- ***What has made this new birth into a living hope possible? Look again at verse 3 and find two things – one flows from the other.***

Jesus' resurrection really *is* the event which changes everything. The penalty for sin is death. That is what we deserve. But Jesus died to pay for all our sins. His resurrection confirms that the penalty for sin has been paid in full.

Because of Jesus' death and resurrection, God can treat us with great mercy. Mercy means not getting the punishment we deserve. Because of Jesus' resurrection, what awaits us now is not death but life. We can be confident that we will share Christ's resurrection life. Praise God!

We have been given new birth. We have begun. But there is so much more to come.

PRAY

Praise God that in his great mercy he has given you new birth into a living hope through Jesus' resurrection.

DAY 6

READ 1 Peter 1:4b–5

As you think about the future, what are you hoping for? We mark special days on our calendars. We look forward to them. We make plans. We hope everything will go well.

Sometimes it does. Sometimes it doesn't. We think we are in control, but really the idea that we can control the future is a mirage. Is there anything we can be sure of?

Peter's word to us here is a resounding yes! Peter looks into the future of these Christians and sees something that is absolutely certain. It is certain for you too if you are trusting Christ. God has given believers new birth into an inheritance.

- ***What reassuring facts does Peter tell us about our inheritance (v. 4)?***

Peter tells us that our inheritance is being 'kept' for us. We can't see our inheritance now but it is real and nothing can spoil it. God is keeping it safe for us in heaven. God has a rich future planned for us that nothing can touch.

- ***Our inheritance is being kept safe for us. But what else is being kept safe according to verse 5, and how?***

Our inheritance is safe, but are *we* safe? Peter reassures his Christian readers. They are being 'shielded by God's power' until God's great salvation is revealed on the last day.

This does not mean God will shield Christians from all suffering now, but God *will* save them. On judgment day believers will be saved from the punishment their sins deserve. On that day, the full extent of God's anger against sin and the full wonder of Jesus' salvation will be clear to everyone. That great salvation is sorted and certain. It will be unveiled on the last day. As Peter says, it 'is ready to be revealed in the last time' (v. 5).

How does God keep us safe for that great day? God keeps us safe by keeping us trusting Jesus. If you have your faith in Jesus today, it is a sign. It shows that God is keeping you safe spiritually. On the last day, you won't miss out. You will receive the great salvation God has planned for you. You will receive that inheritance which can never perish, spoil or fade. Praise God!

PRAY

Thank God that he is keeping your inheritance safe for you, and you safe for it, as you keep trusting Christ.

DAY 7

READ 1 Peter 1:6

What kind of day will you have today? As we look at our lives, we tend to divide our days into happy days and sad days, with maybe some days which are just plain ordinary in between. But in today's verse Peter speaks about his readers having two very different emotions at the same time.

- ***What is causing these Christians grief? What is causing them to rejoice?***

To understand why these believers are rejoicing, we need to read back over verses 1–5. Jesus has died and risen. These believers in Jesus have been cleansed from their sins. God's salvation is coming. God's inheritance is coming, and nothing can spoil it. There are so many good things! Peter wrote because he wanted to encourage his friends. He wanted to tell them again about the true grace of God. Here it is!

Peter has pointed these Christians to gospel certainties. These truths are like solid rocks under their feet as stormy trials rage. These are things of which they can be sure. We can be sure of them too if we have put our faith in Christ. Whatever else is happening to us, these wonderful facts are still true. We can remind ourselves of these truths and rejoice in them even in dark and difficult times.

It seems that Peter's readers *were* experiencing dark times. Stresses and difficulties were piling up. They 'have had to suffer grief in *all kinds* of trials' (v. 6, my italics).

- ***How long would these griefs and trials go on?***

Does Peter mean that none of his friends' problems would last more than a week or so? As we read on, this does not seem to be what Peter expects.

The 'now' Peter refers to seems to be this present age up until Jesus returns. Peter is encouraging his readers to get a sense of perspective. Jesus is coming. Then they will live with Jesus *forever*. Then they will enjoy their glorious inheritance *forever*. Compared with *forever*, our times of trouble in this life will, one day, seem like just 'a little while'.

God is very powerful, so why doesn't he shield us from these difficulties now? He could do that. Why doesn't he? Peter is going to tell us some of the reasons. We will look at these tomorrow.

PRAY

Whatever kind of day you have today, ask God to help you rejoice in all he has done for you and all he has promised you.

DAY 8

READ 1 Peter 1:7

Suffering is very hard to understand and very hard to live with. The Bible doesn't answer all our questions about suffering. There is much we do not know now. But we can be sure of this: God has not abandoned us. In fact, God promises to be at work for our good even in the midst of trials.

- ***Why have these trials come (v. 7)?***

Trials show up what we really believe. Peter pictures our faith as being like gold and our sufferings as being like fire. Fire does not destroy gold, if it's real gold. And trials will not destroy our faith in Jesus, if it is genuine. If we keep on trusting Jesus when things are tough, it shows that our faith in him is real.

Fire does something else to gold too. It burns away all the impurities, leaving just the precious metal. Put gold in fire and, in the end, all you will have is pure gold.

In a similar way, God can use our difficulties to strengthen and purify our faith in him. When we lose other things, it can help us rely on Jesus more. Trials can help us see that our only real security lies in Jesus. They can help us cling to Jesus even more closely. Perhaps you know the reality of that yourself?

Of course, we do need to respond to trials in the right way. We need to run towards God for help and not away from him. When the heat is on, we need to ask God to help us do that.

Gold is precious but our faith in Jesus is far more valuable. Our faith is the means God uses to keep us safe until he takes us home on the last day. The yellow metal we put in bank vaults now will not last into eternity. But our relationship with Christ will be precious forever. Nothing is more important. Peter wants us to look at our trials from the perspective of eternity.

- ***What will the good result of all this be on the last day?***

On that day, it won't be gold which is shining gloriously. Jesus will be seen as he really is. He will be glorified. Our faith in him will be part of that.

PRAY

Ask God to strengthen and refine your faith in him when you encounter trials.

DAY 9

READ 1 Peter 1:8–9

What's it like being a Christian? So far, in his letter, Peter has told these Christians a lot about their future. They have a marvellous inheritance coming. They have a great salvation coming. Their present sufferings will have a wonderful outcome 'when Jesus Christ is revealed' (1:7). But Jesus Christ has not been revealed yet. The world cannot see Jesus now and neither can these believers.

So many of the good things about being a Christian lie in the future. But the best thing about being a Christian has already begun. At the heart of being a Christian, both now and in eternity, is our relationship with Jesus Christ.

- ***What is unusual about our relationship with Jesus now (v. 8)?***

Peter himself had known Jesus personally while Jesus was on earth. But Peter's Christian readers, like us today, had never seen Jesus. Yet these people loved Jesus and believed in him. They had put their trust in someone they had never seen. That has been the experience of every Christian from that time on, right up to today. We have been chosen 'to be obedient to Jesus Christ' (1:2). We know that Jesus is Lord. But Jesus is not some distant ruler we seldom think about; he is the person we love most in the world.

- ***Why are these Christians full of great joy (vv. 8–9)?***

The answer is surprising. Peter has just been talking about salvation as a future event – 'ready to be revealed in the last time' (1:5). Yet here he speaks of believers rejoicing because they are *already* receiving salvation. These Christians certainly weren't being rescued by God out of all their current troubles. So what does Peter mean?

Think of it this way. God's plan of salvation may not be finished yet, but it has begun. Now, today, that plan is moving forward and we are a part of that.

What does it look like today to be part of God's plan? The answer is that it looks like a very mixed bag. Believers have the joy of trusting and loving Christ, but they also suffer trials. This is what God's salvation looks like in the present.

Are you loving and trusting Christ in the midst of suffering? Then be reassured. You *are* being saved.

PRAY

Ask God to help you rejoice in loving Jesus today and in being part of his great plan of salvation.

DAY 10

READ 1 Peter 1:10–12

Peter's readers are filled with joy, even in the midst of their sufferings. They love Jesus and they are receiving his salvation. In today's verses Peter has more to tell his friends about this salvation. He wants them to see more of the wonder of the gospel.

When you are suffering, it is easy to wish you were somewhere else. Peter wants his friends to see how blessed they are to be exactly where they are. How blessed they are to know Jesus and all he has done! The great prophets of Old Testament days knew something about the Christ who was coming. But Christians know so much more!

In verses 10–11, Peter tells us some remarkable things about these prophets of long ago. He tells us that the Spirit of Christ was speaking through their words. The Spirit in them told of the grace which Christ would bring to believers. The Spirit spoke too about Christ's sufferings and the glories which would follow.

- ***Who were these Old Testament prophets serving (v. 12)?***

These prophets wrote about the Messiah, they longed to know more about him, but they never knew Jesus themselves. Peter says that their words about the coming Messiah were not written to help them. These prophets were writing to serve Christian believers.

And their words do help us. It is very reassuring to know that God planned his great salvation so long ago. It is reassuring to know that everything God planned is on track. Christ's suffering was not a surprise; it was not an accident. God said it would happen and it did. God said that glories would follow, so we can be sure of that too – for Christ and for us.

- ***So, as we read the Old Testament, the Spirit is pointing us to Jesus. How else is the Spirit pointing people to Jesus now (v. 12)?***

Peter says that God sends his Holy Spirit from heaven to speak through human preachers of the gospel. When you heard the gospel message, you heard a human person speaking. But God's Spirit was also at work in that encounter. That is an amazing thought. It was the Spirit himself who pointed you to Christ and his gospel of grace.

Even angels long to know more about this glorious gospel. How hugely privileged we are to know it!

PRAY

Ask God to help you appreciate how privileged you are to know Christ and his salvation.

DAY 11

READ 1 Peter 1:13

'Therefore ...' This is the next word Peter writes. In verses 1–12, Peter has been laying out some of the great truths of the Christian gospel. Now he will tell his believing friends what they should actually do in the light of all this.

Peter has told these believers who they are and where they are heading. They are God's chosen people. They are on their way to a glorious future. These things are certain. Next Peter will tell us how Christians should travel to their glorious inheritance, their 'promised land'.

First, Peter speaks about what goes on in our heads. This is vital. It determines everything else we do.

- ***What should our minds be like (v. 13)?***

The Greek word that the NIV has translated as 'alert' has the idea of being in gear, ready to move. As believers in Christ, we need to get our thinking ready for action and change. God has rescued us, but we aren't home yet. We have many trials to negotiate on the way home. We have a spiritual journey to make to our promised land. We can't have our minds in bedroom slippers. Our thinking needs to be in tough, laced-up hiking boots. We need to be ready to move! Our thinking needs to be 'fully sober' too. We need to keep our destination clearly in view so that we stay on track.

- ***What is the destination we must 'set [our] hope on'?***

We don't see Jesus yet, but one day we will. On that day, those who love and trust Jesus will receive his grace. By his grace, we will escape the judgment our sins deserve and will receive the glorious inheritance he has promised us. We need to keep that day constantly in our sights. That is our destination. We need to set our hearts on it.

How will we keep going as Christians? What happens in our minds is vital. We need to get our thinking geared up for action. We need to keep our focus on the finishing line and set our hearts on getting there. Then we will get moving, and keep moving. We will avoid distractions and pitfalls. We will stay on course.

What have you set your hope on? Whatever it is, it will shape how you live today.

PRAY

Pray that you would set your hope on the grace that is coming.

DAY 12

READ 1 Peter 1:14–17

Peter urges his Christian readers to live as 'obedient children ...' God 'has given us new birth' (1:3). It is new birth into his own family. God is now our father. Children are to obey their earthly fathers. How much more should this be so with you and your heavenly Father.

- ***Peter tells his friends three ways this obedience should work out in practice. What are his three commands (vv. 14, 15, 17)? (Notice how Peter gives a reason for each one.)***

First, these believers must stop obeying their old sinful desires (v. 14). These 'evil desires' belong to the bad old days when these believers didn't know God. In those days of 'ignorance', they just followed whatever sinful desires bubbled up in their hearts. But now they are children of God and they must obey him instead.

There is always a clash between what God wants and what sinful human beings want. Every thought, every action is a choice. Who will you choose to obey today?

The second command is,to 'be holy' (v. 15). These believers' lives used to be a mirror of the sin in their hearts. Now their lives should be a mirror of God's holiness. Human children look like their parents; Christians should look like their Father too. God wants us to be just as pure and good as he is. Our home is with him.

Thirdly, we must live 'in reverent fear' of God (v. 17). We need to do that because of the sort of judge God is.

- ***How does God, our Father, judge each person's work?***

Our Father is holy (v. 16). He hates all evil. He is also a perfectly just judge. He is impartial (v. 17). God may be our father, but that doesn't mean he has lower standards for us, just because we are in his family.

Wonderfully, God forgives our sin through Jesus' death, but we are still to 'live ... in reverent fear' of him (v. 17). God still hates sin. He wants us to stop it! We are not to settle down in disobedience. We can't presume to slip all kinds of sinful behaviour past God, as if he will just look the other way.

Being obedient children sounds like a big ask, but did you notice the word 'call' in these verses? God has called us into relationship with him and he invites us to call on him to help us live as he wants.

PRAY

Call on your Father to help you obey him today rather than your old sinful desires.

DAY 13

READ 1 Peter 1:18–19a

'Precious'. We reflect on this word today. 'Precious' means more than just 'valuable'. It means valuable to you personally. Something precious is something very dear to your heart.

- ***What does Peter describe as precious (v. 19)?***

This is a strange thing to say about the violent death of a friend, but Peter wants his readers to see just how precious Jesus' blood is and why. It will help them live 'in reverent fear' (1:17).

- ***What has Christ's blood done (vv. 18–19)?***

Jesus' blood has redeemed us. To redeem means to buy or to buy back. Peter seems to have the Old Testament story of the Passover in his mind here. God redeemed his Old Testament people out of slavery in Egypt by the death of the Passover lambs. This pointed forward to Jesus' saving death on the cross.

Jesus' blood has now bought these believers out of an 'empty way of life' (v. 18). That does not mean Peter's readers used to have blank diaries and nothing to do. They were probably very busy, doing life the way it had been done in their families for generations. But they did not know the God who made them. They were slaves to their own evil desires. They were trapped in a way of life which would end only in God's judgment on their sin. Back then they were not God's children. Back then they had no glorious future. But things are very different now.

How much do you think you are worth? Jesus was willing to pay an enormously costly price to buy you out of spiritual slavery and make you his own. Jesus paid with his own blood. In Bible times, slaves were usually redeemed with silver or gold. We think of silver and gold as valuable, yet their value is fleeting; it won't last forever. But the future God has planned for believers will never perish; it will last for eternity. All the silver and gold in the world could not buy what Jesus' blood bought for us. No wonder Peter calls Jesus' blood 'precious'!

Peter's point is very clear. His message is: look what it cost Jesus to buy you freedom from that old way of living. Don't take Jesus' blood lightly. Don't go back to your old ways. Live your new life. Live it in reverent fear!

PRAY

Ask God to help you see how precious Jesus' blood is and to live the new life his blood has bought for you.

DAY 14

READ 1 Peter 1:19b–21

God's plan to save us is simply extraordinary. Peter has been telling his friends about the precious blood of Christ which has redeemed them, and he has more to say.

- ***What does Peter call Christ (v. 19)?***

A 'lamb without blemish or defect' was sacrificed in each household on Passover night. God planned the Passover Lamb to be a visual aid, pointing forward to Jesus and his death for sins. Like the Passover Lamb, Jesus was perfect. He did not deserve any punishment. Jesus died for our sins; he had none of his own.

Long ago in Egypt, careful preparations had to be made for the Passover. The lamb had to be chosen seven days before the night of God's great rescue. But Jesus, the true Passover Lamb, 'was chosen before the creation of the world' (v. 20). Jesus' death was not God's 'plan B'. God has been planning our rescue through Jesus since forever.

With the coming of Jesus, God's plan has gone public. God has revealed his Messiah to the world. Jesus walked the streets of Palestine. He taught great crowds. He died in front of Roman soldiers. His resurrection was witnessed by hundreds. If you had been alive then, you could have seen it all. God has made it perfectly clear that Jesus is his chosen Messiah and he has done it for our sake (v. 20). Just as in Egypt long ago, Christ, God's perfect Passover 'Lamb', has brought freedom from slavery and a glorious inheritance to God's chosen ones.

- ***In the next verse Peter tells us more about this new life and new future. What does Peter say about how we live now (v. 21)?***

This is all about trust. Who or what we trust will shape how we live. Peter's readers used to have faith in the ideas their ancestors passed down to them. But this way of life was empty; it had no future.

Christ's death has brought us to trust in the only person who is fully trustworthy. Now we trust God and this trust will shape everything we do.

This is the God who raised Jesus from the dead and glorified him. Because of Jesus, we can look into the future with great confidence. After Jesus had suffered, God 'glorified him' (v. 21). God will do the same for us too.

PRAY

Praise God for Christ, our perfect Passover Lamb, and for God's eternal plan to save us through his precious blood.

DAY 15

READ 1 Peter 1:22–25

'Love one another deeply, from the heart' (v. 22). Today's verses revolve around this one central command. We have been redeemed from our old way of living by the precious blood of Christ. We have begun a new life, and loving one another is right at the heart of it.

- ***Peter begins by explaining why believers love one another. How has this happened (v. 22)?***

Peter writes of a new obedience, which leads to a new purity, which leads to a new love. This is a description of the beginning of the Christian life.

Obedience is the right response to hearing the truth about the Lord Jesus. Christians are those who have been 'chosen ... to be obedient to Jesus Christ and sprinkled with his blood' (1:2). We have been purified by his blood. Now we are called to a new life of purity, living as obedient children.

We leave behind our old ways and begin a new life together. In this new family, the bond of love between us is real. It flows naturally out of becoming a Christian. Now Peter calls on believers to *keep* loving. We must love one another 'deeply, from the heart', whatever happens.

- ***Many things will put this love under pressure, but we must keep loving each other. Why must we (vv. 23–24)?***

We should love one another because we 'have been born again'. When a baby is born, a new life begins. We have been born again spiritually, so now we must live our new life together as God's redeemed people.

This new life will last forever. That is what Peter stresses here. We have been born again through 'the living and enduring word of God' (v. 23). It is this 'imperishable' seed which has brought us new life.

Peter contrasts this 'seed' with 'perishable seed'. Our physical human life begins from a perishable seed. However glorious human lives seem now, they are soon gone, like the bloom of a flower (v. 24). But the word of God, which has been preached to Peter's Christian readers and to us, is eternal. The new life this word brings is eternal too. So, love your Christian brothers and sisters! The relationships in our new family will last forever. Let's make them good ones!

PRAY

Ask God to help you to keep loving your fellow believers deeply and from the heart, whatever happens.

DAY 16

READ 1 Peter 2:1–3

How can we keep good relationships good? God's enduring word brings new birth into new relationships. Peter wants these new relationships to endure too. But it is hard to keep loving relationships good. You probably know that first-hand!

- ***Sin wrecks relationships. If these Christians are going to grow loving relationships which last, what must they do (2:1)?***

They must get rid of any desire to harm each other. Slander, and the malice which prompts it, must go. These believers must get rid of all envy and hypocrisy too. Bitterness and spiritual one-upmanship will sprout and flourish from these dangerous seeds. Yet how easy it is to wish we had what others have or to pretend we are better than we are. Christian brothers and sisters must love each other deeply and get rid of anything that will spoil this love.

- ***What else does Peter want his friends to do and why (v. 2)?***

Peter wants them to crave spiritual food. Literally, he tells these believers to crave pure 'wordy' milk or 'the pure milk of the word'.

Newborn babies cry out for milk. Babies will not settle until their hunger is satisfied. It is vital for their life; they will not live and thrive without it. Christians need the spiritual food of God's word. Our hearts are to cry out for God's word as babies cry out for milk.

Christians are born again through God's word (1:23). Peter's friends have begun the Christian life. They have 'tasted' the goodness of God in the gospel (2:3). Now they need to keep feasting on that life-giving word. Only then will they grow up in their salvation. The same is true for us today.

How is your spiritual hunger for God's word? Spiritual hunger works differently from physical hunger. With physical hunger, the more you eat, the less hungry you feel. But spiritual hunger works the other way round. The more you eat, the more spiritually hungry you feel.

So, if you aren't feeling spiritually hungry, if you aren't craving pure 'wordy' milk, it is a sure sign that you need to get on and eat something! Get listening to God's word again. That is the way to feel more hungry spiritually. Try it!

PRAY

Pray you would crave the spiritual food of God's word so that you will feed on it and 'grow up in your salvation'.

DAY 17

READ 1 Peter 2:4–5a

If you have put your faith in Jesus Christ, you are a person with a glorious future, but your privileges are not all in the future. Peter wants to show his Christian readers more about what they have now.

Peter has been calling on his friends to keep craving the 'spiritual milk' of the Lord's word (2:2). As Christians engage with Christ's word, they are engaging with Christ himself. They are *coming* to him (v. 4). We can't see Jesus yet, but we can encounter him today as we hear his word and respond rightly to it. Let's keep coming to Jesus!

- ***We come to Jesus – that is what we do. But what is God doing as we do that (v. 5)?***

God is at work on a building project. We are 'being built into a spiritual house'. Peter pictures Jesus as 'the living Stone' and Christians as 'living stones' (vv. 4–5). God is joining us to Jesus and to each other to make something new and hugely important. Peter will use lots of other images from the old Jerusalem temple to explain this.

- ***What does Peter want these believers to know about Jesus, 'the living Stone' (v. 4)?***

Here are two different views of Jesus. God sees Jesus as precious. He is God's chosen one. But when Jesus came to earth, people did not choose Jesus. They rejected him. They didn't treat him as precious at all.

Peter wants to reassure his Christian readers. They live amongst people who continue to reject Jesus and his people. Peter wants these believers to know that in choosing Jesus and seeing him as precious, they are on God's side. That is the side to be on. People rejected Jesus. They killed him. But Jesus is not dead now. He is the *living* stone. He is the living foundation of God's new community.

We, together with Christ, are being built into a new temple, a new spiritual house, where God lives by his Spirit. If we can, we choose our homes with great care. They are very important to us. It is a tremendous privilege to be part of the place God chooses to make his home!

PRAY

Thank God that he is building us, 'like living stones', into a spiritual house where he chooses to dwell.

DAY 18

READ 1 Peter 2:5b

Where should you go if you want to meet God? In Old Testament times, the right answer to that question was Jerusalem. Back in those days, God was present in a special way in his temple in that great city.

But that is not true anymore. Today you will find God living in the spiritual community of Christian believers. No wonder we need to get on with loving each other deeply and getting rid of all malice! When outsiders visit God's new 'temple', they need to see God's love in action.

In this section of his letter, Peter is weaving together lots of images from the old Jerusalem temple. He wants to show his Christian friends how Jesus is fulfilling everything from those days. Today we learn more about why God has joined us to Christ and to each other as 'living stones'.

- ***What is the purpose of the 'spiritual house' God is building (v. 5)?***

We are 'to be a holy priesthood'. In Old Testament days, only a few special people were chosen to be priests in God's temple. Look how different things are now: the whole Christian community that God is building is his holy priesthood. We, together, are to bring God to people and people to God.

Old Testament priests offered physical sacrifices of animals. This symbolised the fact that our sin deserves the death penalty. Now there are no more *physical* sacrifices. Jesus' blood paid for all sin, past, present and future.

But that doesn't mean that we, God's new priesthood, have nothing to do. We have 'spiritual sacrifices' to offer and Peter will tell us more about these as we read on. For now, though, notice that whatever we do for God should not make us proud.

- ***Why does God find what we do for him 'acceptable'?***

God doesn't accept our service because it is perfectly pure and holy. It never is, so stay very humble. Yet God does accept it and God does accept us 'through Jesus Christ', through his death for us.

God has great purposes for us to fulfil. We are 'living stones' in the most important meeting place in the world. We are part of a 'holy priesthood'. We have the great privilege of helping others come to know the living God.

PRAY

Thank God for the privilege of being part of God's new 'holy priesthood', helping to bring God to people and people to God.

DAY 19

READ 1 Peter 2:6–8

God is at work on a building project. He is building a community of people who trust in Christ. Now we learn that this new 'temple' was foretold by God's prophets long ago.

The prophet Isaiah pictures God working on a building site in Zion, another name for Jerusalem (v. 6). God is laying a 'cornerstone'. This is the first stone in a building's foundation. Christ is God's 'chosen and precious cornerstone'. God's whole new temple depends on him.

- ***What do we learn about those who trust in Jesus, this 'cornerstone' (v. 6–7)?***

Jesus is not just precious to God; he has become precious to believers too. On the last day, those who trust in Jesus 'will never be put to shame'.

But what of those who reject Jesus? In verses 7–8 Peter quotes two more sentences from the Old Testament about stones or rocks. The apostle sees both sentences as pointing forward to Jesus.

- ***What do we learn here about people's reactions to Jesus and why our response to him matters?***

In the first sentence (v. 7) unbelievers are pictured as builders. They are picking stones to use in making their building. One stone they throw away; they don't want it. But look! This stone will be used. It seems as if one day these unbelievers will turn round and see that they have been building the wrong building entirely. The stone they rejected as useless has become the cornerstone of another building. It is the foundation stone of the building that God is building for himself to live in.

In the second sentence (v. 8) we learn that this rock or stone will be the downfall of some people. To Christians, Jesus is the precious cornerstone. Believers are building their lives on Jesus. To us, Jesus is good news. But Jesus is not good news for everyone. It all depends on how you respond to him. To those disobeying him, Jesus is like a boulder in their path that makes them trip and fall headlong to their doom.

Do you see Jesus as precious or useless? Will you come to him in worship and obedience, or will you reject him? It matters now because it will matter a very great deal in eternity.

PRAY

Thank God that those who trust in Jesus will not 'be put to shame' and pray for those you know who need to stop rejecting him.

DAY 20

READ 1 Peter 2:9–10

'But you ...' Here is a great and a wonderful contrast! Those who disobey the message about Christ are in a terrible situation, as Peter as just made clear. But how different things are for you, if you have trusted in Christ. Today's verses are the climax of all that Peter has been saying about God's new people. He wants his friends to be gloriously clear who they are and what great purposes God has for them.

Before they became believers, Peter's readers were in a bleak state. Look how the apostle describes it in verse 9. Darkness is a picture of being far from God, ignorant of him and under his judgment. All of us once lived in this darkness. We were separated from God and from each other. We were 'not a people' (v. 10), that is, we had no significant status or identity. We were just spiritual nobodies! And we had not received the mercy from God which we so desperately need. But now everything is different. Peter wants to stress just how different.

- ***What has happened to us and who are we now (vv. 9–10)?***

God has been so kind to us. We have been chosen, called and given mercy. And we deserve none of it! Living in darkness is over. Now we live each day in the glorious light of God's presence and favour.

All the privileges of God's Old Testament people of Israel now belong to us. We are God's 'chosen people', his 'holy nation' and his 'special possession'. What was true for Peter's first readers is true for us too, if we are trusting Christ. We have received so much grace!

Like the nation of Israel in Old Testament days, we too are a people with a purpose. God chose us for a reason. With our privileges comes a great responsibility.

- ***What does Peter say here about God's purposes for his new chosen people (v. 9)?***

We are to make plain what God has done. We are to 'declare' God's praises. We are to speak of the wonder of God's grace to others.

Back in 2:5, we learnt that we are 'to be a holy priesthood, offering spiritual sacrifices'. Now Peter begins to tell us what this new 'priesthood' is to do. How will we bring God to people and people to God? We are to tell others what God has done so that they may come to worship him too.

God wants our praise to well up from our hearts and to reach our lips. How will you speak of him today?

PRAY

Ask God to help you declare his praises so that others may see his glorious grace.

DAY 21

READ 1 Peter 2:11–12

We have been chosen by God to declare his praises (2:9). We need to speak of his grace in Christ. But how we live matters too. Our lives can draw people to listen to our words about Jesus, or they can put people off. Yes, our lives really matter. Peter wants his friends to be very clear on this.

- ***First, what does Peter urge his dear friends to say no to and why (v. 11)?***

Peter is very realistic! He knows believers are tempted to behave just like everyone else. But we are 'foreigner and exiles' here in this world. We need to look different.

We need to say no to our sinful desires. That is what 'abstain' means. Giving in to these desires can ruin us spiritually. These desires 'wage war' against our souls. We need to take this very seriously.

- ***Then secondly, what does Peter call on these Christians to do and why (v. 12)?***

Peter wants the lives of his friends to be full of 'good deeds' which are obvious to everyone. He wants their good deeds to speak so loudly that they flatly contradict those who accuse Christians of doing wrong.

Peter's vision is bigger than that though. He doesn't just want pagans to stop making false accusations against God's people. Peter wants these unbelievers to begin to glorify God themselves (v. 12). Peter wants these outsiders to be safe on the last day when God 'visits' his world in judgement. Christians are to declare God's praises but Peter wants unbelievers to come to worship him too.

We need to be careful here! It is possible for believers to live good lives but not be amongst pagans. Christians can retreat into a kind of Christian ghetto. Our lives may be full of good deeds but no unbelievers ever get to see them.

It is also possible for Christians to be out amongst the pagans but not be living good lives. It is possible to be thoroughly involved in the world around us but be thoroughly compromised too. The danger here is that we live lives which are no different from anyone else.

We need to live *good* lives *amongst* the pagans. Will your life today help people want to know more about Jesus? Or less?

PRAY

Ask God to help you say no to sinful desires and to live a clearly good life so that others may want to glorify him too.

DAY 22

READ 1 Peter 2:13–15

How does God want us to live today? God calls us to live good lives 'among the pagans'. This will help them begin to glorify God too (2:12).

Peter wants his friends to know how this will work out in practice, so he gives them a big principle to guide them. We look at this principle today. Peter will then go on to apply this command to all sorts of everyday situations.

- ***What does Peter want his Christian friends to do, 'for the Lord's sake' (v. 13)?***

Peter began his letter by telling his readers that God had chosen them 'to be obedient to Jesus Christ' (1:2). Now Peter tells his friends that if they want to obey the Lord Jesus, they must 'submit ... to every human authority' too. Being submissive to people in authority is one of the distinctive marks of living as a Christian, as Peter will show.

- ***What is God's aim in asking Christians to do this (v. 15)?***

Peter calls submitting to human authorities 'doing good'. It is one of the 'good deeds' unbelievers are to see on display in our lives (2:12). Peter helps us see why this submission is so closely linked to 'doing good'.

He mentions some examples of human rulers (v. 13). These rulers run systems of justice for their citizens. That is true whether the rulers are believers or not. Murderers, thieves and other wrongdoers get punished while those who work for the good of society get honoured. So submitting to human authorities, being a law-abiding citizen, will usually cash out as 'doing good' in a way which is public and obvious.

This is a big part of God's strategy for silencing the criticisms of foolish and ignorant people (v. 15). God's strategy to silence criticism isn't shout louder. It is live better.

Of course, not all human rulers are good rulers. Sometimes there may be a direct clash between a command of a human ruler and the commands of God. Peter was once in just this situation. You can read about it in Acts chapter 4. Peter was clear that it is always right to obey God rather than human beings in such cases (Acts 4:18–20).

But unless there is such a clash, believers are to submit, for the Lord's sake, to every human authority. Think what that will look like for you today.

PRAY

Ask God to help you be submissive to human authorities for the Lord's sake.

DAY 23

READ 1 Peter 2:16–17

Peter has just told his friends to submit to every human authority, 'for the Lord's sake' (2:13). Now Peter has more to say about how to think about this submission. He uses the language of freedom and slavery.

- ***How should believers live (v. 16)?***

Christians are to live as free people and also as God's slaves. What does this mean? A free person has the right to choose how he behaves. A slave is someone who belongs to his master and owes him total obedience.

Human authorities do not ultimately control how believers behave. We do not belong to them. In this sense all Christians are free. We are free to choose to obey human authorities, and we should. But we are also free to choose *not* to obey them, if needs be. Sometimes obeying human authorities will involve disobeying God. Our first loyalty is always to him. We belong to God and we are to live as his 'slaves'.

The bottom line is that believers answer to God. We should fear his displeasure more than we fear earthly punishments. A fear of people is replaced by a fear of God. And that is very liberating!

- ***We are free to choose but what must Christians avoid choosing (v. 16)?***

Christians must not use their freedom to choose as an excuse to do wrong. We are not to break the laws of the land without good reason and then excuse ourselves by saying that these laws don't apply to us. Instead, we should use our freedom to relate to everyone in a way which pleases God.

Peter gives us a number of examples of this in verse 17. Some of these commands are about how to relate to God and God's family: we are to 'fear God' and 'love the family of believers'. Other commands include unbelievers too: 'honour the emperor' and 'show proper respect to everyone'.

Peter interleaves these different sorts of commands to show his friends that God is concerned about all their relationships. There is an appropriate way for believers to behave in every relationship – in church, in work, in the family and in society.

Who will you meet today? How will you treat them? How will living as 'God's slave' work out in your relationships today?

PRAY

Ask God to help you choose to live as his 'slave' today, aiming to obey him in everything.

READ 1 Peter 2:18–23

Living good lives involves being submissive to human authorities. Peter now takes this general principle and applies it to the workplace of his day.

Slavery was the most common work situation back then and it was a very mixed experience. Often slaves were treated more like servants or employees, but not always. Peter isn't approving slavery of any kind here. But if Christians find themselves as slaves, Peter wants them to be good workers, not bad ones.

Then, as now, not all bosses were fair and kind. But Christian workers are still to be submissive to those in authority over them (v. 18). This is a big ask!

Peter lifts these believers' gaze to look beyond their human masters. Read through today's passage and look for all the times Peter refers to God. Our relationship with God changes how we see everything.

Slaves were to submit to their earthly masters not because they feared them, but because they feared God. They were to be conscious of God as they worked and to seek his commendation. In the workplace, as in all of life, God's verdict on what we do is the one that matters most..

- ***Whose example should Christians follow and what will this look like (vv. 20–23)?***

Believers will suffer unjustly at times. When that happens, Christ's example is the model we should follow. Jesus also suffered unjust punishment when he died on the cross. Jesus was completely perfect and sinless (v. 22), yet the rulers of his day punished him.

When Jesus was insulted with words and hurt in body, he did not hit back. He did not make threats. He endured it. Look at the end of verse 23. Jesus put himself in the hands of God, the perfect judge. Jesus trusted that God would judge justly and would punish all sin on the last day. When we face injustice, we can have the same confidence.

Slaves in those days had few rights and few options. But they could choose to work well, even when badly treated, and trust God to punish all injustice on the last day.

Today believers may have more options. We may be able to appeal for justice (as Paul did in Acts 25:11). But we don't always get justice. Nor is it is always possible to leave a bad employer. In these situations, Christians should continue to do good work. Like Jesus, we too can entrust the situation to God. He will judge justly on the last day.

PRAY

Ask God to help you work well today and to follow Christ's example if you are treated unjustly.

DAY 25

READ Isaiah 53:5–12

Peter writes with his mind full of Old Testament scriptures. We read a section of these scriptures today. The prophet Isaiah foretells the coming of Jesus. He describes him as a servant who would suffer unjustly at the hands of others.

Peter has been addressing Christian slaves or servants who also suffer unjustly. They are to follow the example of Jesus, the suffering servant, and not hurl insults back at those who harm them. But Jesus' suffering does not just give us an example to follow; Peter has already told his readers that 'Christ suffered *for you*' (1 Pet. 2:21, my italics).

Much of Peter's understanding of Jesus' death and resurrection seems to flow from Isaiah's prophecy. Peter sees the person and work of Jesus reflected very clearly in Isaiah's words. Isaiah speaks about God's 'righteous servant' who was without sin (Is. 53:11) and without 'deceit' (v. 9); Peter recognises that this is Jesus (1 Pet. 2:22). This perfect, sinless servant of God suffered unjustly, but he did not retaliate (v. 7).

- ***God's suffering servant was righteous. But what does Isaiah say about all of us (v. 6)?***

When we look in the mirror, we may look quite respectable, but really we are just like wilful sheep. We have gone miles off the path of righteousness. Each of us has deliberately turned away to follow our own sinful desires. The reality is that we are far from home and in great danger.

- ***But the suffering of God's righteous servant brings us hope. Why did this servant suffer (vv. 5–6, 11–12)?***

These verses speak of a wonderful exchange. The LORD laid on this righteous servant the sin of us all. Jesus bore the sin and iniquity of many. He took the punishment our sins deserved. And we, the sinful ones, received peace with God. Our broken relationship with God was restored.

As for God's righteous servant, after he had suffered, he would 'see the light of life' (v. 11). Suffering now, glory to follow – we have seen this pattern many times now!

Take some time to reflect on Jesus' suffering for you. We need to stand back in awe and wonder at God's gracious plan of salvation, foretold in such detail so many centuries before. Tomorrow we will look at how Peter uses Isaiah's words to help us understand more.

PRAY

Thank God that Jesus was willing to suffer for your sins to bring you peace.

DAY 26

READ 1 Peter 2:24–25

Long ago Isaiah wrote remarkable words about a righteous servant of God. This servant would die to bear our sin before seeing again 'the light of life' (Is. 53:11). Isaiah also wrote about our great need. We were all like sheep gone astray. But the wounds of this servant would bring wonderful change for us.

Peter is clear that this servant is Jesus Christ. Peter's words about Jesus in today's verses again echo Isaiah's prophecy. Jesus' death accomplished something extraordinary. He endured the death penalty our sins deserved. He was punished in our place. He 'bore our sins' as he died (1 Pet. 2:24). Jesus' death changes everything for those who trust and follow him.

- ***What does Peter say about our new relationship to sin and righteousness (v. 24)?***

Sinful desires still rise up in our hearts, clamouring for our attention. But when they do, it must be as if they are trying to attract the attention of a corpse. It must be like trying to provoke a dead body. We are to be completely unresponsive to their pleas for us to do wrong.

Jesus died to put an end to sin's consequences for us on judgement day, but he also died to end sin's presence in our lives now. Instead we are now to 'live for righteousness'.

People live for all kinds of things. But believers are to walk through each day on the lookout for every opportunity to do what is pleasing to our righteous Lord. Our aim now is to follow in his footsteps.

- ***What more does Peter say about the change Jesus' death has brought us (vv. 24–25)?***

Christian servants or slaves back then probably knew all about wounds. Like Jesus, they were sometimes beaten for wrongs they did not commit. But God is always at work for good, even in the midst of suffering. God brought great good out of Jesus' wounds. Our relationship with God was healed by his suffering.

Peter's picture in verse 25 is of coming back to where we should be. Sheep belong under the caring rule of their shepherd. And through Christ's death we have come back to God, our shepherd. We have returned to that relationship of submission and security for which we were made. We have come home.

Jesus died to bring you back to God, to live under his loving rule. Live your new life today.

PRAY

Thank God that Jesus bore your sins so that you might die to sin and live for righteousness.

DAY 27

READ 1 Peter 3:1–6

Submission means choosing to allow someone else to lead you. It is not a popular idea today. But, rightly understood, submission is one of the distinctive marks of Christian living.

Believers have been chosen to be obedient to Christ (1:2). We are to submit for the Lord's sake to every human authority (2:13). So citizens should submit to their governors, servants to their bosses (2:18) and here wives should submit to their husbands (3:1).

- ***What good effect can this have (vv. 1–2)?***

Sadly, some Christian women are married to men who have heard the gospel message but rejected it. How can these wives help their husbands move towards faith in Christ? Peter wants the behaviour of these women to do the talking in their homes. That is the best way of commending the gospel to these men. Peter wants husbands to see purity and reverence in the lives of their wives.

- ***Peter talks about two kinds of beauty here. What does he say about each kind (vv. 3–6)?***

One kind of beauty depends on adding various things to our outward appearance. The other kind of beauty depends on what is happening in our hearts and is 'of great worth in God's sight' (v. 4). This inner beauty is the only kind of beauty which lasts. Peter says it is 'unfading'.

Part of this inner beauty is having 'a gentle and quiet spirit' (v. 4). This has nothing to do with being shy. Peter is continuing his theme of believers choosing to be submissive. In scripture, God calls on husbands to love their wives and give a caring lead in their families (see Eph. 5:25–33). How will Christian wives respond to this loving leadership? They may be tempted to dismiss it, undermine it, fight it or just grumble about it. But Peter wants believing wives instead to have a quietness of spirit that chooses to be submissive. Marriage the way God intended is a beautiful thing. It mirrors the relationship of Christ with his beloved church. It is a visual aid of the gospel.

Wives' submission to their own husbands is not a new idea (v. 5). This is exactly the sort of beauty that holy women, like Sarah, have always pursued. Peter describes this as doing 'what is right' (v. 6). He wants Christian wives to fearlessly follow her example.

PRAY

Ask God to help Christian wives to be submissive to their own husbands and to value inner beauty as God does.

DAY 28

READ 1 Peter 3:7

Christian wives are to choose to be submissive to their husbands. Peter's command may raise many questions in modern minds. Does Peter see wives as inferior in some way? Will choosing this path of submission benefit the husband and harm the wife? We need to read on.

- ***How should Christian husbands behave (v. 7)?***

The word the NIV translates as 'considerate' includes the ideas of being a student and also of being a blessing. Each Christian husband is to become a student of the needs of his wife. He is to consider carefully what is best for her. Every husband needs to become an expert in knowing how to bring blessing to the particular woman he has married. Bringing her blessing is to be his aim in all he does.

Peter tells Christian husbands two truths about their wives which will help them see how they should treat their spouses.

- ***What does Peter want Christian husbands to know about their wives (v. 7)?***

Peter tells Christian men to remember that their wives are their partners. They are not inferior in any way. They are not their servants to order about. But why does Peter describe wives as the 'weaker partner'?

In a relationship, if one partner chooses to submit to the other, that submissive partner is choosing a role of potential vulnerability or weakness. Peter is reminding husbands here that they must never misuse their wife's godly submission. They must never take selfish advantage of their leadership role in marriage. Instead, husbands should honour their wives' godly behaviour.

Husbands should also treat their wives with respect because they are 'heirs with [them] of the gracious gift of life'. In Peter's day, usually only sons inherited the wealth of a family. But in God's new family, both men and women can look forward to the glorious future life Peter spoke of in chapter 1.

Spiritually speaking, husbands and wives share a level playing field. Both are equally made in God's image, equally in need of God grace and equally heirs of God's gracious gift of life.

So husbands need to stay very humble as they lead and care for their wives. God cares greatly how we behave at home. Husbands must not think their spiritual lives will thrive if they are treating their wives badly. Listen to Peter's warning!

PRAY

Ask God to help Christian husbands to be considerate, respectful and prayerful as they live with their wives.

READ 1 Peter 3:8–9

'Finally, all of you ...' Peter has spoken to slaves, to wives and to husbands. Now the apostle wants to speak to all of his Christian readers.

Peter will give us some golden rules for all Christian relationships. He will tell us the keys to building good relationships and how to respond when sin spoils things.

- ***What do we learn here about Christian relationships (v. 8)?***

Peter begins by reminding his friends of the unity they share. To 'be like-minded' means literally to be of one mind. This does not mean that Christians must agree on everything, from hobbies to holiday destinations. But we must stay of one mind on what is most important of all. We need to stay focused on the great truths of the gospel that we share. We have been called together to obey Jesus Christ. We are travelling together to our glorious inheritance. We must stay together!

Next, Peter speaks about how we must care for one another. Sympathy, love and compassion are to be hallmarks of our relationships. We are not to look inwards, just taken up with our own concerns. We need to walk with our brothers and sisters, sharing their pains and being there to comfort and support them. We need to help each other keep going.

Humility is vital for good relationships too. The proud person thinks he is always right and seldom apologises. Pride has a poisonous effect on relationships. The humble person remembers his own need of God's grace and is quick to pass it on. Humility in relationships is like gold dust.

But what about when relationships go wrong? All personal relationships involve getting hurt sometimes. The desire to give as good as we get may well up inside us. Yet we must interrupt that downward spiral of repaying evil with evil. We must 'repay evil with blessing' (v. 9). That is how God in his grace has treated us. We need to treat others in the same way.

- ***Why else should Christians behave like this (v. 9)?***

God has called us to turn from evil and to do good. We are called to be just like our heavenly Father as we relate to one another. We are to pass on the grace we have received. This is the way to great blessing. Let's respond to God's call.

PRAY

Ask God to help you be loving and gracious to others, just as he has been to you.

DAY 30

READ 1 Peter 3:10–14

Peter has been telling his Christian readers how to inherit a blessing. Believers are to heed God's call to turn away from evil and to do good. This is the way God's chosen people have always been called to live.

In Old Testament times, King David suffered greatly but he carried on trusting and obeying God. Peter quotes David's words here, taken from one of his psalms. David tells his children the way to live God's good life. Words matter (v. 10). Watch what you say. Keep control of your tongue. Say nothing false or deceitful.

Actions matter (v. 11). When the desire to do wrong wells up inside you, don't listen that nagging voice. Choose to do good instead.

Relationships matter (v. 11). Don't let anything wreck them. Pursue peace. Run hard after it; don't let it get away! Don't give up. Keep looking for reconciliation.

This sounds a very attractive list. You would think that anyone would welcome these qualities in their neighbour or employee. Much of the time you would be right! As Peter comments in verse 13, 'Who is going to harm you if you are eager to do good?' But you would not be right all the time.

- ***What may happen to you, despite your good life (v. 14)?***

Suffering and threats sound unpleasant and frightening. But those who do good are still 'blessed'. We may not feel very blessed when we are suffering. David's words help us see why we are blessed, even when in the midst of trials.

- ***What does David say about God (v. 12)?***

You are blessed because God's face is turned towards you in favour. God notices when you keep your tongue from evil. He sees when you do good. When you forgive and seek peace, God is watching. He cares about what you do. His ears are attentive to your prayers for help. Things may be tough now, but in the future faithful believers will certainly see good days! Terrifyingly though, God has set his face against those who do wrong. On the last day God, will destroy all evil. Doing wrong has a bleak future.

You will have many opportunities to choose to do right today, and when you do good, God sees. He is listening out for your prayers for help, so cry to him. And be assured you have his blessing.

PRAY

Thank God that his eyes 'are on the righteous and his ears are attentive to their prayer' (v. 12). Ask him for help to do what is right today.

DAY 31

READ 1 Peter 3:14b–16

We are to live good lives for God. But we are also to speak about him and his grace. Otherwise good lives will only bring glory to those who live them. So now Peter returns to the subject of speaking.

We already know that we are to declare the praises of God, but Peter wants to make clear that this will not be easy.

- ***What do we learn here about how unbelievers may respond to us?***

We may hear all kinds of painful words spoken against us: slander, threats and unjust accusations.

- ***How should believers respond (v. 14)?***

First, believers need to decide who to fear. How we behave will always depend on who or what we fear most.

Peter tells his Christian readers to fear or 'revere Christ as Lord' in their hearts (v. 15). This is crucial. Those who threaten and slander Christians may look very powerful, but their power is limited and temporary. Jesus Christ is risen from the dead and he is Lord. He has authority over what happens to everyone in eternity. We need to remember that.

Secondly, Peter tells these believers that they need to be prepared to speak of their hope in Christ (v.15). When we are opposed and threatened, we may be tempted to say as little as possible about our faith. But Peter's words challenge that reaction. Peter says we must always be ready to give people answers to their questions, so we need to think about what we will say.

Peter assumes here that the way Christians live will raise questions in people's minds.

Thirdly, Peter tells his Christian readers *how* they should speak (vv. 15–16). Everything about the way we speak should make the Christian message attractive. It should reflect what God is like. Believers should answer 'with gentleness and respect'. The manner of explaining God's grace needs to be gracious! Believers should *always* be ready to answer *everyone*. God's generous offer of grace is open all hours to all people everywhere.

We must also keep 'a clear conscience'. Our 'good behaviour in Christ' should display God's goodness and contradict slander.

Living good lives and explaining God's grace need to go hand in hand. It is not a case of choosing one or the other. God's chosen people need to do both.

PRAY

Pray you would revere Christ as Lord and always be ready to explain your faith in him.

DAY 32

READ 1 Peter 3:17–18

Are you likely to suffer for being a Christian? Peter clearly sees suffering as part of normal Christian experience.

Christians may be taken to court and imprisoned for living out their faith in Christ. That has happened to believers all through history. But Christians should not suffer because they have done wrong. They should not be in court because they are guilty of murder, theft and the like.

- ***When we suffer for our faith, we may be tempted to think that God has abandoned us. But what does Peter say about God's control (v. 17)?***

However powerful our opponents may look, things are not out of God's control. God has not been sidelined. Even our unjust suffering is under God's ultimate control. It is not outside his will.

God can use even such suffering for our good and for his glory. Peter has made this clear already in his letter. Now he points his Christian readers to the time God did that in the most wonderful way of all. Christians are not the only ones who suffer for doing good. They follow a Lord who suffered even though he was righteous.

- ***Peter reminds us here of the purpose of Jesus' suffering. He also tells us more about what Jesus' death achieved. How does Peter explain this purpose (v. 18)?***

Jesus did not suffer for his own sins – he had none. Jesus suffered for the sins of the unrighteous – that is all of us. Christ bore the penalty for our sins so that we will not have to. Christ died once to pay the price for all sins – past, present and future.

Peter tells his Christian readers that Jesus did this 'to bring you to God'. Jesus died to restore our broken relationship with God. Reflect on all that Jesus did for you – his pure, undeserved grace.

Peter wants to encourage his suffering readers. Jesus suffered for doing good – look how God used that! Through that suffering, Christ brought you to God. Christians still suffer for doing good, but God can use that suffering too to bring more people to himself.

That is not all. Jesus' physical suffering and death was followed by his glorious resurrection and ascension. He was 'made alive in the Spirit' (v. 18). Suffering now, glory to come – Peter has stressed this pattern again and again in his letter. This was Jesus' experience. It will be the experience of Jesus' followers too. We are to reflect on this and be encouraged.

PRAY

Praise God that Christ died for sins, once for all, to bring you to God.

DAY 33

READ 1 Peter 3:19–22

Peter is reflecting on Jesus' resurrection and all that it means. Today's verses begin and end with this great fact.

- ***Where is Jesus Christ now (v. 22)?***

Peter's readers are being opposed and threatened. But Peter wants these believers to be clear that the risen and ascended Jesus Christ *is* Lord of all. Angels, authorities and powers are in submission under him, even though it doesn't look like that now.

Peter wants to reassure his friends, so he points them to another time in Bible history when evil was raging. In Noah's day, there were evil spiritual forces at work (v. 20). Then, too, it looked as if God was doing nothing about this wickedness. But God was not careless; God was waiting – waiting patiently until his plan to judge evil and save his people was ready. When Noah had finished building the ark, God kept his promise. Evil was judged. God's people were saved as the ark rose up to the top of the flood waters.

What about believers now? In our time, too, evil seems to flourish, but Jesus' resurrection should reassure us. First, Jesus' resurrection confirms that evil will be defeated and judged. Powers and authorities are in submission to the risen Christ. In verses 19–20, Peter tells us more about some of these powers. He writes of spirits who were disobedient back in the days of Noah. The risen Jesus 'went and made proclamation' to these forces of evil. These evil spirits were not destroyed yet but they were imprisoned. It seems most likely the risen Christ declared to them his victory over all evil powers. His resurrection signed and sealed their final destruction.

Secondly, Jesus' resurrection means that we will be saved. In verses 20–21 Peter again takes us back to the days of Noah. Coming up through water to salvation, as the ark did, is a picture of what happens to Christians when they are baptised.

Believers are baptised at the start of their Christian life. It is a sign of our salvation. The point of baptism isn't to wash your body. Peter calls baptism a 'pledge'. It is an acted-out promise. Baptism is a promise from God that we will have a clear conscience before him on judgment day. God will keep his promise to us, just as he did to Noah.

- ***This great salvation rests entirely on what Jesus has done. Peter comes back to this point once again. How does salvation come to us (v. 21)?***

Our salvation rests on the resurrection of Jesus Christ from the dead.

PRAY

Pray that Jesus' resurrection would give you great reassurance today.

DAY 34

READ 1 Peter 4:1–2

Christ suffered on his way to glory. Christians will suffer too.

It was God's will for Jesus to suffer and Jesus submitted to that. Christians need to 'arm' themselves with this same submissive attitude (v. 1).

If we need to 'arm' ourselves, it must mean that we have entered a danger zone. Sinful desires 'wage war' against our souls (2:11). This battle is especially intense when we are suffering. We will be strongly tempted to live 'for evil human desires' (v. 2). If following Christ involves suffering, we will be tempted to deny and abandon our Lord.

Jesus was tempted to avoid the cross too. Yet he submitted to his Father's will, even though that involved suffering (see Matt. 26:39). We need to think like Jesus. Remembering Jesus' example and sacrifice will strengthen us.

- ***How will suffering for Christ change a faithful Christian for the better (v. 1)?***

If you have suffered for your Christian faith, it will change you. In particular, suffering can change how you see your sin. Peter says that 'whoever suffers in the body has finished with sin'.

- ***What will being 'finished with sin' look like in practice (v. 2)?***

Suffering for Christ helps us make a radical break with living for ourselves. When we suffer for Christ, we experience first-hand something of what it cost Christ to 'finish with' the *penalty* for our sin. How can we see what it cost Jesus to 'finish with' our sin and then continue to flirt or compromise with it? We will want to be rid of it!

Suffering for Christ also raises an important question very starkly: whose side are you really on? When you submit to suffering for Christ, it is like decisively burning all the boats of living your old life. It is clear that you *do* no longer live 'for evil human desires'. There can be no doubt now where you stand. You are 'finished with' sin.

When we experience suffering for following Christ, we *will* be different afterwards. We do not instantly become perfect, but as we learn to submit to God's will in the crucible of suffering, we will change. If we obey God on that hard day, we will want to obey him on all the days that follow too.

PRAY

Jesus always lived to obey his Father's will. Pray that suffering for Christ would help you live to do this too.

READ 1 Peter 4:3–6

Becoming a Christian means changing. We stop living for 'evil human desires' (v. 2) and start living for God's will.

In verse 3 Peter gives a shocking catalogue of sinful behaviour. This is how these believers used to behave. They had worshipped idols rather than God. But things are very different now.

- ***How do unbelievers respond to the way Christians live (v. 4)?***

Unbelievers are not just surprised, they are also hostile. When people change, others can feel criticised. They may retaliate. Unbelievers are heaping abuse on Peter's Christian readers. It can be very hard to be on the receiving end of all this.

But Peter wants his Christian friends to keep going at living for the will of God. He wants them to see what really matters. So he points them forward to what is coming.

- ***What will happen to those who 'heap abuse' on Christians (v. 4)?***

Unbelievers may live recklessly now, but a day of reckoning is coming. Jesus the judge will hold them to account for their sin and their idolatry. No one will escape Jesus' judgment. He will judge everyone. Jesus 'is ready to judge the living and the dead'.

Judgment day is on its way. This day motivates us to keep preaching the gospel, even if it brings suffering to those who accept it. God's final verdict on us is far more significant than what people make of us now.

This is what Peter seems to be reflecting on in verse 6. He appears to be thinking about Christians who have suffered for their faith and have now died. These believers have experienced two very different 'judgments'.

One judgment does not ultimately matter. Unbelievers judge Christians according to sinful 'human standards' and may condemn them. But unbelievers can only hurt our physical bodies. The other judgment is the one that matters. The verdict on believers 'according to God' is very different. On the last day these dead Christians will, like Jesus, be made alive in the spirit. God will have the last word.

So keep going at living to please God, however costly it is. People may misunderstand you and heap abuse on you. You may even lose your life now. But you will not lose your life in eternity.

PRAY

Pray you would remember that Jesus is coming to judge everyone and that his verdict on you is the only one that matters.

DAY 36

READ 1 Peter 4:7

There is only one salvation event left on God's calendar. Jesus 'is ready to judge the living and the dead' (4:5). We don't know when that day of judgment and salvation will be. It could be any time. Jesus is ready to come. We need to be ready for his coming.

- ***The world as we know it will not last forever. How does Peter describe 'the end of all things' (v. 7)?***

We must not mentally park Jesus' second coming on some distant horizon in our thinking. We must not forget about it. We need to keep Jesus' coming at the forefront of our minds. Peter says it is 'near'. That is how we should think of it.

How we think is so important. Three times in this letter Peter calls on his readers to be alert and sober in their thinking. He must believe that this is very important!

The opposite of being sober-minded is thinking like someone who is drunk. When someone is drunk they are out of touch with reality and out of control. They may lose any clear grasp of who they are and where they are. They may be unaware of dangers which surround them. They may sleepwalk straight into all sorts of risk and difficulty.

Peter does not want his friends to go through life thinking like a drunk. He wants them to keep their thinking clear. We need to stay switched on to reality. Jesus is coming. It will happen. It could be anytime. When we see that clearly, it will change how we see everything else. We won't lose sight of what is most important: that we keep trusting and following Jesus, and that we help others do that too.

- ***What effect will staying alert have?***

One reason we don't pray is that we get distracted by all sorts of things. Our heads buzz with the urgent and we lose sight of the important. But when we are thinking clearly, we will remember what is coming. We mustn't give up on speaking about Jesus. We mustn't give up on following him, despite the suffering that will bring. How much we need God's help to keep going!

So don't be muddle-headed in your spiritual thinking. Remember that Jesus' coming is near. Remember how dependent you are on God. Cry to him for help. Pray!

PRAY

Pray you would stay alert and prayerful, remembering that the end of all things is near.

DAY 37

READ 1 Peter 4:8

These days we have highlighter pens. We can underline words or type in bold. We have lots of ways we can show that something is really important. In Peter's day, if you wanted to emphasise something, you repeated it. And repeated it again. And again. In today's verse, Peter repeats another command he has given before: 'love each other deeply'. This is vital too.

- ***In fact, loving each other deeply must stay right at the top of our list of priorities. Which little phrase tells us that (v. 8)?***

There are lots of things that can trip us up spiritually. But Peter seems to think that bad relationships within the church family may be the most dangerous of all. 'Above all', we must keep loving each other deeply.

- ***What does Peter say here about why believers should 'love each other deeply'?***

We will encounter 'a multitude of sins' as we relate to one another in the church family. Sin always puts relationships under pressure. I want my way. You want yours. I behave badly. You do too. Selfishness, pride and bad temper so easily tear us apart. What can stop relationships within God's family being destroyed by sin? Peter's answer is love, for 'love covers over a multitude of sins'. When something is covered over, you can't see it anymore. If my sins are covered over, you won't look at them any longer.

What do you see when you look at your brother or sister in Christ? Do you just see a long list of all the ways that person has hurt you and wronged you? Maybe you can scarcely see the person Christ loved and died for anymore. Yet that is how we should see one another. Above everything else, we must love one another deeply. When we do that, we will be quick to be gracious and quick to forgive.

Our love for each other does not pay for our sins – only Christ's death does that. But God loved us enough to treat us with grace, and we are to love enough to pass that grace on to each another. We are to stop counting sins against one another. We are to stop keeping a record of wrongs. The way we love each other should remind people of the way Christ has loved us.

PRAY

Thank God that love can cover a multitude of sins. Pray that would be a reality in your life and in your church family.

DAY 38

READ 1 Peter 4:9–11

Above all, believers must love one another deeply. Everything else about Christian relationships flows from loving like this. Now Peter tells us more about how this works out in practice.

He begins with hospitality (v. 9). Welcoming others into our homes can be a great joy, but it can be costly too. It is easy to grumble about it. Being hospitable can be thoroughly inconvenient at times. As a joker once put it, 'The art of hospitality is making people feel at home when you wish they were!' But God has generously and ungrudgingly welcomed us. God has been hospitable to us. We are to mirror this in the way we treat each other.

God has been so generous to us. Every believer has received God's grace. We are freely forgiven through Christ's death. But that is not the end of God's generosity. He gives every believer other gifts too.

- ***How should Christians use 'whatever gift' they have received (v. 10)?***

God gives his people many different free gifts, but all of them are to be used for serving others, not our own egos. We are to be 'faithful stewards of God's grace in its various forms'. A steward looks after something which is owned by someone else. These gifts from God continue to belong to him, so we must use them as God wants.

Peter's concern is that 'in all things God may be praised through Jesus Christ' (v. 11). Believers must use their gifts for God's glory and Peter shows them how.

How should those gifted at speaking and serving use their gifts? Speakers, remember that it is God's word that you are relaying as you preach. You are passing on 'the very words of God'. Any power you have comes entirely from passing on God's word in scripture, not your own ideas. Be dependent. Be humble.

If you are gifted at serving, you will need God's strength to serve well. Again, be dependent. Be humble. So, if you are feeling proud or self-sufficient, you need a reality check! But if you are feeling inadequate, be encouraged! God doesn't just give us gifts and walk away. He gives us strength to use them.

In love God has welcomed us and served us. The way we relate to each other should reflect how God has treated us. And in all we do, we are to seek his glory.

PRAY

Pray all this would be true in the life of your church family.

DAY 39

READ 1 Peter 4:12–13

There will always be days when being a Christian seems very hard. Peter wants his friends to respond in the right way on those days.

- ***What reaction must these Christians avoid at such times (v. 12)?***

If you are a believer in Jesus, you should expect flack. Peter has made this clear before and he does not minimise how hard this suffering will be. He calls it a 'fiery ordeal'. We will feel pain. But we should not feel surprise.

There may be a temptation to feel surprise though. Peter has just been extolling God's eternal power and glory (4:11). Why doesn't God use his great power to protect his children from ordeals, particularly fiery ones? That might seem both strange and surprising.

Peter wants his friends to understand why God lets his people go through the mill. These sufferings are not purposeless. One purpose is that they act as tests (v. 12). As we persevere, these trials show that our faith is real, and they make our faith stronger. God is at work for our good, even in the toughest of times.

- ***If we are not to be surprised by suffering, how are we to respond to it and why (v. 13)?***

Can Peter be serious? A 'fiery ordeal' sounds far from enjoyable. We need to read on. These believers are to rejoice because of what their suffering means. Peter tells us to rejoice 'as you participate in the sufferings of Christ'.

Peter does not mean that Jesus' death to save us was inadequate. Christ's perfect sacrifice for sin does not need to be topped up by our sufferings. But when Christians suffer for following Christ, they are walking the path Jesus walked. In that sense, suffering can be strangely reassuring. It can assure us that we genuinely belong to Christ. We really are walking in his footsteps.

All suffering is painful at the time. But 'inasmuch' as it shows we belong to Christ, we can count it as a joy. Suffering led to glory for Christ. It will lead there for Christ's followers too.

One day Christ's glory will be revealed. It will be clear for all to see. On that day, faithful followers of Christ will 'be overjoyed'. On that glorious day, our suffering will be over and our joy will be overwhelming.

PRAY

Pray that you would see your sufferings as 'participating in the sufferings of Christ' and would rejoice in this reassuring truth.

DAY 40

READ 1 Peter 4:14–16

How does it feel when others mock you for being a Christian? It is easy to feel isolated and downhearted. We can feel that God has abandoned us. Again, Peter wants his believing friends to see their sufferings differently.

- ***Unbelievers may be cursing you for your faith, but what does Peter say is true about you (v. 14)?***

Jesus told his followers, 'Blessed are you when people insult you ... because of me' (Matt. 5:11). To be blessed is the exact opposite of being cursed. How is God blessing you when others mock and sneer? Look where God is when 'you are insulted because of the name of Christ'. As the insults rain down on your head, God's Spirit of glory will be resting on you too.

God is actually very close to you when you suffer for Christ. God's Spirit rests on you, just as he did on Jesus when he faced suffering (Matt. 3:16 – 4:1). How reassuring it is to know that!

The Spirit of God is also the Spirit of glory (v. 14). Being a Christian often doesn't look very glorious now, but God's Spirit is already with us, guaranteeing the glory that is coming. Yes, we are blessed.

- ***Of course, Christians should never get grief because they are guilty of doing wrong (v. 15). But how should believers respond to suffering for being Christian (v. 16)?***

Being known as a Christian can feel like a hard 'label' to wear. People may mock and scoff. But Peter's message is don't be ashamed of the name 'Christian', even if it brings you suffering. See it differently.

When you hear someone's name, it tells you which family they belong to. You bear your family's name. Christians bear the name of Christ. By his grace, we sinners belong to him. This is astounding. God is willing to link our names with the great name of Jesus Christ, his Son.

People may call us 'Christian' in sneering tones, but we need to hear that word 'Christian' in a different way. To be called a 'Christian' is always a wonder of grace. It should lead our hearts to well up with praise to God.

PRAY

Thank God for the privilege of bearing the name of his dear Son and for the blessing of the Spirit's presence. Pray you would never be ashamed of the name 'Christian'.

DAY 41

READ 1 Peter 4:17–19

Being known as a Christian will sometimes bring us great suffering, But Peter wants his friends to 'praise God' (4:16).

- ***Why should they do that (v. 17)?***

God's timetable is right on track and this time of suffering for God's people has a place in God's plan. '... it is time', Peter says. These sufferings have a purpose too. They are working 'judgment' on God's own household.

God is using these trials to sift out and destroy sin amongst his own people. This is not a judgment of condemnation but of purging and cleansing. We are to praise God that we are numbered amongst the holy people he is saving.

God's prophets looked forward to the time when God would judge sin and end all evil. They said God would start by disciplining and refining his own people (see Mal. 3:1–4).

But this is only the beginning of God's action again evil. A much worse time is coming for those who 'do not obey the gospel of God'.

- ***What two questions does Peter ask his readers to help them reflect on this (vv. 17–18)?***

Peter's point is this: if God's righteous people suffer now as he disciplines them, how much worse will it be for the ungodly when God turns his attention to them. Even the people God is saving experience hardships now. How much worse it will be on the last day for those who are heading for destruction.

- ***How does Peter want his friends to respond to all this (v. 19)?***

When Jesus suffered unjustly, 'he entrusted himself to him who judges justly' (2:23). Jesus trusted God to punish those who were causing his suffering. Jesus did not give up doing what was right. Peter wants his suffering friends to respond as Jesus did. They too should commit themselves to God and continue to do good.

If 'part one' of God's plan is happening now, we can be sure that 'part two' of God's plan is coming down the track. God *will* judge and destroy all his enemies. Things are not out of control, however they may seem. This is God's world; he is our faithful creator; we can rely on him to keep his promises.

God will save his people. So trust your way to him and press on!

PRAY

Pray you would trust God and keep pressing on, and pray for those you know who do not yet obey the gospel of God.

DAY 42

READ 1 Peter 5:1–2a

When unbelievers give Christians a tough time, church leaders tend to get the worst of it. And authority always brings its own pressures and temptations too.

Believers must 'continue to do good' (4:19), despite their suffering. Peter will tell his friends how this should work out in practice and he begins with leaders.

Peter appeals to 'the elders among you' (v. 1). This is a serious call. Senior Christians in the congregation must step up and take responsibility. They need to be willing to lead, despite the flack.

Peter begins by pointing them to his own experience of leadership.

- ***What does Peter say about himself, about his own experience and about his hope for the future (v. 1)?***

Peter calls himself 'a fellow elder'. Of course Peter is not only an elder; he is also an apostle. But Peter's message here to these church leaders seems to be: I walk where you walk; I know how tough it is to lead and care for God's people; I understand. Peter also calls himself 'a witness of Christ's sufferings'. Godly leadership has always involved suffering. Christ our leader suffered before entering glory – Peter knew that first-hand. Christ's leaders should not expect it to be any different for them. But Peter is also expecting to 'share in the glory to be revealed'. Peter does not want these elders to forget what will follow their sufferings. Christian leadership will not bring honour and glory now, but glory is coming.

- ***Now Peter turns to address the elders directly. What does he call on them to do (v. 2)?***

'... "you were like sheep going astray," but now you have returned to the Shepherd and Overseer of your souls' (2:25). Peter has pictured Christians as a flock of sheep. The Lord is now our leader and protector.

But these human elders are also to shepherd this flock. They are to watch over and care for these 'sheep'. Yet those under their care do not belong to them; this is 'God's flock' (v. 2). This fact colours everything elders do. Elders must keep the Lord's precious ones safe until he comes (5:4). So, elders, shepherd these 'sheep'. Don't lose even one. Step up to the plate! This really matters.

PRAY

Pray the leaders in your church would shepherd God's flock courageously and faithfully through every suffering and difficulty.

DAY 43

READ 1 Peter 5:2b–4

What makes a good leader? Peter is speaking to elders in the church family. He wants them to shepherd God's flock. Now he tells them how they should lead.

You will be reminded of Jesus here. These elders are to model themselves on Christ, the 'Chief Shepherd' (v. 4). They are to avoid the pitfalls of power and they are to do good.

- ***What is the first danger to avoid and good to pursue (v. 2)?***

Jesus said, 'No one takes [my life] from me, but I lay it down of my own accord' (John 10:18). Jesus, the good shepherd, willingly laid down his life for his sheep. Christian leaders too are to be willing carers, not resentful conscripts. God wants that.

- ***What is the second danger to avoid and good to pursue (v. 2)?***

Jesus said, 'the Son of Man did not come to be served, but to serve, and to give his life as a ransom for many' (Mark 10:45). So, elders, be eager to serve too. Leading God's flock is about giving not getting. Keep asking, 'What can I give?' not, 'What's in it for me?' Elders must not be self-serving or corrupt. They must never use their position to pursue 'dishonest gain'.

- ***What is the third danger to avoid and good to pursue (v. 3)?***

Power brings many temptations. Dishonest gain is one temptation. Lording it over others is another. But elders are not to lead in this way. They are not to arrogantly push people around. They are not to seek glory for themselves. That was not the way Jesus led.

Jesus humbly served his disciples. He even washed their feet and then told them, 'I have set you an example that you should do as I have done for you' (John 13:15). Jesus showed people the way to live by living that way himself. That is how Christian leaders are to lead too.

All in all, watching over God's flock sounds a tough job. But Peter gives these leaders a great encouragement: Jesus, the Chief Shepherd, is coming to take his flock home (v. 4). The elders' job may be tough but it is temporary. Elders won't be honoured now for what they do, but they will be honoured then. Their suffering won't last but 'the crown of glory' will be theirs for keeps.

Is it worth stepping up and shepherding God's flock? Is it worth keeping going? Christ kept going. He served through suffering all the way to glory. Follow your leader.

PRAY

Pray for your church leaders, that in every way they would follow Jesus' example in the way they lead.

DAY 44

READ 1 Peter 5:5–6

How easy are you to lead? Being a good leader is hard. Being a good follower has its challenges as well.

Leaders are not to lord it over those entrusted to their care. They are to serve. Leaders are to lead with humility. Followers are to follow with humility too.

Those of us who are younger must decide to be submissive (v. 5). That will be hard, especially on days when we think we know better. But we are not to be stroppy or try to take over. We are to be easy to lead.

- ***Who needs to 'clothe' themselves in humility and why (v. 5)?***

Every morning when we get up we choose some clothes and put them on. Peter wants believers to choose to put on an attitude of heart too. All Christians are to choose to clothe themselves with humility towards one another.

If you look at a person's body, it is obvious which physical clothes they have picked. If you look at a person's relationships within the church family, it will be obvious if they have chosen to put on humility. Will we act as if our own desires are more important than other people's? Will we act as if we are always right?

Pride is such a dangerous game to play. We may succeed in making ourselves look big in front of others, but the illusion won't last. Our opponent in this game is far bigger. Look who opposes the proud (v. 5). To have God as your enemy is a terrifying prospect. God will humble the proud in judgment on the last day.

- ***What must we do therefore, and why (v. 6)?***

Humble yourselves. Do so yourself before God does it for you! We do not enter the Christian life humbly on our knees before God and then get up and begin to strut. We remain undeserving sinners in desperate need of God's grace. We never graduate from that. God is God and we are not. We do well to remember that.

Those who walk humbly with God will walk humbly with their Christian brothers and sisters too. In the Christian life, the way up is down. God gives his favour to the lowly. Humble yourself now and in God's good time he will 'lift you up'.

PRAY

Ask God to help you clothe yourself with humility as you relate to others in your church family.

DAY 45

READ 1 Peter 5:7

This is a wonderful verse! Peter has nearly finished his letter. He is leaving his friends with a number of commands and promises to keep in their minds.

Peter says these words are for 'all of you' (v. 5). Here are things that will help every one of these suffering Christians to stand fast in the true grace of God. They will help us too.

- ***What does Peter tell his friends to do (v. 7)?***

Peter assumes that his Christian friends will have all kinds of anxieties chasing around their minds. There is certainly much that might make believers feel anxious. We do not yet see God destroying the proud and lifting up the humble (5:5–6). Today the proud are often flying high while humble believers are often at the bottom of the heap. We know that God will 'lift [us] up in due time' (5:6) but that time can seem a long time in coming. We may wonder how much worse things will get. We may wonder how we will cope.

Yet worry does not change our outward circumstances. Worry does not change the future. But anxiety does change our hearts and fill them with pain.

Peter doesn't want that for his friends. He has a better way to respond to troubling times. He tells his friends to cast all their anxieties on God – not just some of their anxieties but all of them.

This is a wonderful invitation. All those anxious 'what ifs' that chase around our heads – we are to give them to God. Take your concerns to God in prayer and leave them with him.

We can hold on to our worries very tightly. We fear that our concerns might get lost in someone else's in tray if we give them away. But Peter says we can pass our concerns over to God with great confidence.

- ***Why can we have this confidence (v. 7)?***

God cares for us, even more than we do ourselves. What is more, he holds the future in his hands.

Peter has just told these Christians how mighty God's hand is (5:6). Now Peter reminds his friends that this mighty hand belongs to one who cares for them. This is a tender and very precious truth. God is awesome and almighty but also our loving Heavenly Father.

PRAY

Thank God that he cares for you. Cast all your anxieties on him.

DAY 46

READ 1 Peter 5:8–9

A roaring lion is pacing around looking for breakfast. He has his eyes on you. Christians live in a world where we have a dangerous enemy still on the prowl.

Christians suffer grief in all kinds of trials. Peter has written about many of these trials already. These trials come from a number of sources. But there is one source that Peter has not mentioned, at least not until now.

- ***What danger is Peter concerned about here (v. 8)?***

We've seen that the unbelieving world is against believers and our own sinful desires wage war against our souls. Now we're told we have an unseen spiritual enemy too. The devil is circling around us, looking for a way to destroy our faith in Christ. Peter's picture of the devil as a hungry roaring lion is meant to make us sit up and take notice. There is terrible danger here. How can we keep safe?

The devil is on the lookout, but Peter says that believers need to be on the lookout too. Again, he calls his friends to: 'Be alert and of sober mind.' Peter wants these Christians to stay faithful to Christ all the way to their glorious inheritance. If they are going to stay safe, they need to stay on their guard.

- ***How else should Christians respond to this threat (v. 9)?***

Here is a roaring lion, eyeing you up, looking hungry – what would you do? Our natural response is probably to run away. But Peter wants his friends to stay put. We resist the devil by standing firm in our faith. We win against our enemy when we don't give up.

The devil is prowling around looking for some way – *any* way – to take us away from Christ. The devil will stir up opposition to Christ and his people. And when we suffer for Christ, the devil may whisper in our ears, 'God doesn't care about you. Why should you care about him?' But Peter has just reminded his friends that God *does* care.

Peter wants to encourage these believers to keep going. He reminds his friends that being under attack for following Christ is normal. All God's children the world over share that experience (v. 9). In a strange way it should actually be reassuring. It shows we are in the family!

PRAY

Ask God to help you resist the devil by standing firm in your faith, whatever happens.

DAY 47

READ 1 Peter 5:10–11

There are so many things to do! Be humble. Stay humble. Stay awake. Stand firm. Stop worrying.

There are lots of things that Peter wants his Christian friends to do, but is it all up to them to keep themselves safe until heaven? It would be scary if it was! Now Peter points his friends to what God has done and will do.

- ***What has 'the God of all grace' already done for these Christians (v. 10)?***

God hasn't just sent a general message to the whole world. Amazingly, God has also 'called you'. This is personal. God has called us to come to him and to be with him forever in glory.

- ***What does 'the God of all grace' promise to do for believers in the future?***

How do you tend to feel when the pressure is on? Words like weak, wobbly and weary may spring to mind. We may feel we are only clinging on to faith in Christ by our fingertips.

Peter wants his friends to know that it won't always be like this. You may never manage to behave much like a spiritual giant now, but one day you will. God is coming. And when he comes, God will make you just the way you have always hoped to be.

Do you see what Peter is saying? It is all God's grace, dear Christian friends. Your salvation depends on God, not on you. God called you. God chose you in Christ to reach his eternal glory. God will get you there. God started your Christian faith and God will finish what he has begun. And God does have the power to deliver. In fact, he has all 'power for ever and ever' (v. 11).

When you are in pain, time seems to pass very slowly. But when we look back on our sufferings from eternal glory, our time in pain will seem like just 'a little while' (v. 10). Compared to eternity, our time of suffering *is* just 'a little while'.

What is the sign that God has called us to be part of his people? We will keep responding rightly to his word. That is how we were born into the Christian life. That is how God keeps us safe as we journey to his eternal glory. So keep obeying his word and put your confidence in the God of all grace.

PRAY

Thank God that he has called you to his eternal glory in Christ and that he will bring you safely home.

DAY 48

READ 1 Peter 5:12–14

Peter's letter is very nearly done. Before he ends, Peter wants to lay out very clearly why he has written to his dear friends. Look over verse 12 once again and remember Peter's purpose.

- ***So, why did Peter write this letter (v. 12)?***

Peter has said so much that is encouraging! He has told his Christian readers about their present privileges as God's chosen ones and the future glories which are coming.

But Peter doesn't just want to make his friends *feel* better. He wants to encourage them to *do* better too. Every privilege of the Christian life has a job description attached. These believers have been chosen to *be* obedient to Jesus Christ.

Peter has written to encourage these believers to live out God's plans and purposes for them. He wants them to declare God's praises and to live such good lives amongst the pagans that those pagans will come to glorify God too.

But living amongst the pagans has its problems. Life as a believer now can be very tough. Peter has also written to testify that 'this is the true grace of God' (v. 12). There is suffering now but there is glory to come. It was that way for Christ; it will be that way for Christians too. They follow in their Lord's footsteps.

- ***What is Peter's very last command to these believers (v. 12)?***

Don't turn tail and run back to your old way of living. Don't keel over under the pressure. You have the true grace of God. Don't give up!

Peter is rooting for his friends, but many others are concerned for them too, as we see in verses 12–14. There is a great deal of brotherly love in these last verses. Peter's readers may feel like strangers in the world, but they have a big Christian family who love them and want to encourage them to keep going.

If Peter's readers thought they had it hard, the church in Rome ('Babylon') probably had it worse. But those believers too have been chosen by God. You can't spot God's chosen ones by the easy lives he organises for them.

Remember, it is not your physical location which matters, but your spiritual one. All believers live 'in Christ' (v. 14). That is what matters. This really is the true grace of God. 'Stand fast in it' (v. 12)!

PRAY

Pray that what you have learnt from Peter's letter would encourage you, reassure you that 'this is the true grace of God' and help you to 'stand fast in it'.

MORE IN THIS SERIES

ROMANS
Momentous News
By David Cook
ISBN: 978-1-906173-24-1

MARK
The Suffering Servant
By Jeremy McQuoid
ISBN: 978-1-906173-55-5

DANIEL
Far From Home
By Justin Mote
ISBN: 978-1-906173-68-5

1 THESSALONIANS
Living for Jesus
By Julia Marsden
ISBN: 978-1-906173-67-8

PHILIPPIANS
Press Towards the Goal
By Kay Mumford
ISBN: 978-1-909611-31-3

GALATIANS
The Life I Now Live
By Peter Mead
ISBN: 978-1-910587-09-6

ACTS
To the Ends of the Earth
By David Cook
ISBN: 978-1-909611-02-3

EZEKIEL
For His Glory
By Peter Lau
ISBN: 978-1-909611-83-2

JOHN
Never Thirst Again
By David Cook
ISBN: 978-1-909611-30-6

and more at... 10 Publishing
a division of 10 of those.com

To place an order call: **0330 2233 423** email: **sales@10ofthose.com**
or order online: **www.10ofthose.com**

J. Marsden
1 PETER
48 UNDATED DEVOTIONS THROUGH THE BOOK OF 1 PETER